LEARNING
TO SWIM

A MEMOIR

ann turner

SCHOLASTIC PRESS
NEW YORK

LIBRARY OF CONGRESS CATALOGING-IN-PUBLICATION DATA
Turner, Ann Warren
Learning to Swim: a memoir / by Ann Turner. — 1st ed.　　　p.　　cm.
Summary: A series of poems convey the feelings of a girl whose sense of joy
and security at the family's summer house is shattered when an older boy
who lives nearby sexually abuses her.
ISBN 0-439-15309-3 (alk. paper)
1. Sexually abused children — Juvenile poetry. 2. Mothers and daughters
— Juvenile poetry. 3. Children's poetry, American. [1. Child sexual abuse
— Poetry. 2. American poetry.] I. Title. PS3570.U665
L43 2000 811'.54 — dc21 99-050396

12　11　10　9　8　7　6　5　4　3　2　1　　　0/0　01　02　03
Printed in the United States of America　　　　　37
First edition, October 2000

The display type was set in Copperplate 33BC and Caflisch Script
MM Swash 640 Bold. The text type was set in 12-point Cochin.
Cover photograph © 2000 by Marc Tauss • Book design by Marijka Kostiw

Very special thanks to

Gerald Schamess, for his insights and support
Tracy Mack, for her sensitive editing
Miriam Silman, M.S.W., Clinical Director
  Victim Services Program at the Mountain
  Comprehensive Care Center in Kentucky
  who read the manuscript and talked of its uses
Joanne Graves, who helped in my healing
My husband, Rick, who supported me and understood

TO MY FAMILY

AND TO ALL THE

BRAVE SURVIVORS

table of contents

Listen, I am trying

to remember everything

because it keeps coming back

like a skunk dog

on the porch

whining to get in,

and I'm afraid

if I don't let it in

it will never

go away.

This is what I remember:

that hot room,

your strange body,

your hands hurting,

and harsh words in my ears

telling me terrible things

would happen

if I ever

told.

But now you can't

find me or reach me

or hurt me ever

again

and once I tell the words

I am going to kick

you off my porch

and learn to breathe

again.

sailing

We are packing the car

to go to the summerhouse

everything is in bits and pieces.

Nicky and I are fighting

over the seat but I

am not moving,

I am sitting on my pink

swimming ring that Daddy says

I don't need anymore

because I am big enough,

old enough,

and fast enough

to swim on my own.

big enough

Daddy opens the door

to the summerhouse

where the air has missed us

all winter and the mice have left

their little black seeds

over everything.

The water has to be coaxed back

into the pipes

and the windows open

with a scrape and a groan.

Mother sighs about the dust.

I press my fingers into it

leaving ten marks like petals

on the kitchen table.

I'm back.

In the shadowy room

where we eat

the sun comes in small

batches, shining on the blue

willowware plates where I think

the people move when we aren't

looking, but now they are covered

with salad and dinner begins.

Grandma says grace, Peter

drops his cup, and Mother laughs.

I think I could stay here

forever in the sun

and the shadows,

here in the house

that I love.

In the pump house
Grandpa takes my hand.
The air is dark and velvety,
only one
beam of yellow shines
through the open door.
The motor purrs and drips,
we speak softly
as if in church
and I love how
my hand is folded
in his.

Nicky and I climb down

the knobby path to Dresser's Pond.

Daddy holds my hand.

"Don't be afraid."

My pink swimming ring

on the grass

used to keep

the black water below.

Now I cannot see my toes

and flail my arms,

churn the water to a froth,

but the water tugs at me

willing me to go under.

Daddy shouts again, "You can do it!"

I kick my feet,

suck in a breath,

and for a moment,

I sail above

the drowned leaves!

We are playing dress-up

on the porch

where the wasps fly.

I am wearing a blue-flowered hat

and a cream dress that

trails around my feet,

Nicky has glasses,

and Peter a vest.

We are grown-ups

with big words in our mouths

and important looks on our faces

and no one

can boss us around.

We are running races

in the meadow

with the kids from down

the street — Kevin, Lonny, Angie —

legs pumping,

hands swinging,

my feet blur

as I pull ahead of

everyone

my breath works

my heart works

my legs work

and I shout

when I win.

Push your feet

against the mucky bottom,

churn your hands

like Mother's mixer,

swing your legs behind

and kick them up and down.

Don't let that water

cover your face,

I holler inside,

and it almost works

except I suck up a snort

of water that blows out

in a great sneeze.

"Good start," Daddy says.

"You're going to be

a fine swimmer."

Kevin, Lonny, and Angie all live

in a little green house

with a fat mother,

hair greasy in her face,

frying donuts,

and their father is thin

and shabby with an open mouth

shouting

we are running away

somehow I am always It

looking for a place to hide

from their feet and their hot

breath going by.

I am hiding in

their garage, the oily one

with the dented car,

and Kevin is running past,

looking for me

with hands that grab,

and Lonny is looking, too,

with his fat wavery lips

like worms that want

to squish on my cheeks,

and they say it's a game

but I am shivery

in the garage

with the smell of oil

all around.

sinking

"I'll read to you,"

Kevin whispers,

"a secret time for us

and never, ever tell."

He takes my hand

and leads me up the stairs.

But in my hot, yellow room

the book falls to the floor

and he jams his hands

inside of me

and takes out his private parts

that I didn't ever know

could look so huge and strange,

telling me to touch him

in a hard, breathless voice,

and I didn't even know

I could say

no.

Grandma asked me to set
the table for supper
with the willowware plates
that I love   I think
I could walk into that safe
blue world
but suddenly, the plate drops
and breaks   Grandma
does not scold,
she takes me on her lap
and rocks me tight.

Daddy drives us to the store

for ice cream the way we've done

a hundred times before,

but suddenly you are there

outside the car,

even your shadow falling

across me

in the backseat

makes me hide in the corner,

all my angles, all my legs,

all of me scuttling

for cover.

I tried to swim

today

thrashing in the water

but clouds covered the

sun   there was no pink

ring to keep me safe,

and I could not keep my head

above water.

Daddy pulled me out,

thumped my back,

and said, "Next time,

Annie, next time."

It is happening again
your hand is out
holding mine
the book is in your other
hand
we are disappearing
up the stairs
and Peter waves to me
from his playpen.
He can't talk so he
can't tell
(I promised not to!)
and after it is all over
I whisper in his
baby ear
and push my face
into the couch cushions
so no one can see.

I am holding it all
inside like when I am sick
and running to find a bathroom
the words are crowding behind
my lips bursting to get out
so bad my lips ache
but I can't. You said no
not ever not nohow
and you bunched your fist
in my face.
But my dolls know,
Jenny, Amanda, and Fuchsia.
At night
I tell them what you did
and they are sad for me
with their wide-open eyes
and surprised mouths.

There are veils

over the high bush blueberries,

like huge white wings

brushing the ground.

Mother and I scrooge under,

tin cans in hand,

and pull the berries down

so fast they rattle

and fill to the brim.

I hate their sour taste

but love being hidden

under the netting

where no one can see

me.

When you lie on me

the world turns black,

the air folds down

like a hot blanket

and spots float

over my head.

I hold my breath

waiting

waiting

to breathe.

Suddenly
I want to scrub
my smudged face,
my ladder-scarred knees,
my baggy shorts with pieces
of breakfast still on them.
Now I brush my teeth
five times a day,
rearrange my dolls
on the bureau,
and at Dresser's Pond
I crouch in the shallow water
and rub all my hidden places
away.

I thought a secret was

a cookie hidden in a hand,

like the one you hold now

as you lead me up the stairs.

My feet drag

they know what is waiting

at the top

but I am too small

to say no

only my body is so

slow   it is waiting

for someone to

notice

I am going away.

My middle is bare.

I cannot see my toes.

The pine makes shadows

where the bugs fly

in ugly dips and drops.

I look behind

at my ring

sitting on the grass.

Daddy says I can do it.

But I feel so skinny and bare

in the shadowy water

without my pink friend.

"Come on, Annie,

what's wrong?"

Daddy holds out his hand

it is not like the other

hand

taking me away but

still I will not go in.

The water looks gloomy

and dark with shadows

I will be swallowed up

the drowned leaves

will cover my mouth.

I ask for my ring back

and sit

on the grass.

People are talking

to me their voices fluttering

like moths   I do not pay

any attention

I am flying out

of my body

to the corner of the room

above the willowware plates.

I will stay here

until it is safe

to come down.

What I love

is taking my brother's hand

and going out to the meadow

with the light golden

on the high grass

and swinging the pail of garbage.

We dig a hole

and dump in grapefruit peels,

eggshells flecked with orange,

and a scatter of tea leaves

inside the dark, wet hole.

And I stamp my feet

and stamp them more

until Nicky says, "Enough."

I am scribbling

with a crayon

on a crinkly piece

of paper

you have a rain of fire

on your head

your arms are

stumps

your feet

burned off

when Mother asks,

"What is it, Annie?"

words fly away

and she looks at me

with worried eyes.

I am the pig

and you are the wolf

waiting at the door

to gobble me up

and chew on my bones,

then spit me out

and nobody is big enough

or fast enough

or sees enough

to keep it from

happening.

I am reading to Peter

on my lap,

my nose in his

wispy hair.

Nothing bad

has ever happened

to him,

except when he threw up

red Jell-O

all over the bathroom floor,

and no one has ever

hurt him.

Only he and my dolls

know,

and he pats my face

with one soft hand.

In the hot room

where I suffocate,

I can't always tell

if it is an arm, a blanket,

or a leg pressing my face.

I turn cold,

as if all the blood ran out

my toes or dripped from my

fingers to the floor below.

Then would someone notice?

Then could I tell?

I am waiting by

the big stone pillars

for Daddy to come home,

the black back of his humped

car to turn in our drive,

the window down

with his hand waving

and the words will float out,

"Annie! I'm home!"

He will open the door

and I will sit beside him

smelling his safe smell

of ink and smoke and aftershave.

I wish my words

were smoke

he could breathe in

then he would

know.

When my cousin Billy

came to visit

and Uncle Ted joked

about how we'd marry

one day,

Billy tried to kiss me

and I backed away

so sudden, so hard

I knocked into the apple tree

and all the people's mouths

made little *o*'s.

No one knew

why I would never kiss

Billy again and never let

anyone's lips ever touch me

again or let their hands

their hot, dry, hard hands

touch me

again.

At night I dream

of swimming,

my arms move smoothly

through the water

it is so easy, so calm,

I am never afraid.

My toes kick

the black water

into a froth

and I am singing,

waving to Daddy

on the shore.

I am laying out my dolls

in their frilly dresses

and wheeling them down the drive

to the stone pillars

where Grandpa leaves small

letters for us

but each time I do

your face looms up inside

like a movie I sit too close

to and I forget my dolls,

the letters,

the ice cream I meant

to lick the drips from

and I hide under

the blueberry bushes.

I hate the color yellow.

I hate limp curtains.

I hate iron bedsteads

and thick boys in shorts.

When I grow up

I will have a green room

with a soft, mounded bed

and white curtains

blowing in the windows.

In my room

there will never be

a thick boy in shorts.

I took the garbage

the whole pail

and dumped it on the porch

kicking the grapefruit

against the stones

grinding the coffee grounds

into the hot boards.

Someone shouted

someone yelled

I do not care

it is time

to make

a mess.

My mother is reading

me stories about elves

and fairies they live

in a green wood with

a soft light all around.

No one seems to marry

and no one wants to kiss

they only run under the full

white moon, singing,

that is what

I want.

I have a knife

in my hand, slicing

beef on the willowware

plate, and I cut harder,

faster, thinking it

is your pink neck

under my blade

and I am cutting you

into little pieces

that I will bury

in the meadow

outside

when there is no moon

and no stars.

She asked me today,

"What book does Kevin read

up in your room?"

My eyes blinked,

my tongue stuck

to the top of my mouth

on the words I'd been waiting

to say

each one hurt

like a splinter

yanked out

and before I was done

she grabbed me up

and we cried

and cried

until

there were no more

words to tell.

swimming

Mother is jamming on

her walking shoes,

jerking the laces tight,

"Annie, stay here.

Kevin will *never* hurt you

again."

She slams out the

door but I am afraid

of the green house

the lips the hands and him.

I wait on the porch

watching

my stomach clenches in

until I see the top of her head

getting bigger, rounder

then all of her running up the drive

her short hair flying,

and when she holds me

her skin burns.

Daddy took my hands
today, swinging me high
over the hurting plants
in Grandma's rock garden
he settled me on his knee
his safe smell was all
around
and he told me he knew
that he was so sorry he would
drink up every bit of water in
Dresser's Pond if that would
make it all unhappen
it can't
every bit of water
is in my eyes
I sit on his warm lap
and put my head
under his chin.

daddy knows

There is an invisible
string tying me to my mother
she does not let me go
out of her
sight
even to the blueberries
where she crouches beside me
and touches me now
and then
her hands are not hard
or dry
or grasping
and my breath makes a quick
stutter
in and out
like a caught animal
suddenly let go.

Grandpa left me a letter
in the old knothole
by the stone pillars.
I reached in and pulled out
the note covered with blue
words:
"You are my fairy girl
with brown curls
and impish smile
and a laugh like a cloud."
For a moment
I felt like one — airy,
light as mist,
floating up the drive.

I sit on my bed

watching the road

through the window

that leads to

the shabby green house

the oily garage   and him.

I hold Amanda tight

in case he runs up

to our house

my stomach hurts my

toes are cold

but no one comes

no one at all

except the mailman

with a packet of letters.

I think

I am safe

for now.

Grandpa walked down

the steep path

to the pond

with my pink ring

on his head,

"to keep the sun off."

I giggled so hard

I forgot to be afraid

sticking my toes

into the dark water.

i forgot to be afraid

Today

I only brushed my teeth

four times.

Today I climbed

the apple tree

and ate a green fruit

under the blowing leaves.

Today when I crouched

in Dresser's Pond

I did not try to rub

myself away.

I am dressing

my dolls in frilly hats

and thick white petticoats,

tugging their underwear

snug around their

waists

so no skin shows.

I am careful,

so gentle,

my hands never hurt

and I am breathing in

the warm

summer air.

We ate hot dogs,

all eight cousins

on the rock wall

swinging our sneakers

against the hard stones.

Seelye ate so much

he threw up.

I sat next to Billy

but jumped and almost fell off

when his bare shoulder

touched mine.

Daddy held my hand
as we scrambled down
the path to Dresser's Pond.
We waded in together,
and I thought of white, bony
things I could not see,
of a lake octopus waiting
to sucker its tentacles
around my skinny legs.
Daddy said,
"You are learning to swim,"
and I let go of his hand.
"I am learning to swim,"
I chanted
and when the bottom
fell away,
I bobbed on top,
my face like a white flower
before me.

We are packing the car,

the wool seats

prick my legs

everything is jammed

into the black trunk.

Daddy swore.

The smoke plumes out

as we bump down

the drive

I look behind

at the windows

of my little room.

Is there a shadow?

Did he come back?

My stomach churns

I grip Nicky's hand

then I see it is only

the curtain shifting

behind the glass.

The house gets smaller,

the car stops at the end

of the drive

I do not turn

to look up the road

at the green house.

Mother puts her hand

on my knee,

her gold ring gleaming

all the way home

like a spell to keep me

safe.

I woke one night

when the wind

was hot

and I thought

I was back

there

and he

was thumping up

the stairs

but it was Daddy

coming into my room,

pulling me out

of the covers

that suffocated me

and crooning to me

in his arms.

Daddy and I went back

when it was cold

to make certain

no pipes were frozen

no wires gnawed through by mice.

In the winter room,

I pulled open my drawer

to a startled squeak!

Nesting in a Kleenex box

were ten pink rolls of hairless flesh

so new, so safe.

The yellow walls looked bleached,

the hopeless curtains

had disappeared,

and he was gone.

I took deep breaths

of the icy air

and bounced

on my clean bed.

Listen.

Telling is what matters.

You have to catch

the words you've been hiding

inside or keeping in a dark

hurting ball in the middle

of your stomach that make you

sick

but pulling the words up

and out, spilling them

across the floor, the table,

dropping them into someone's

surprised face   that

is what matters

and after this time

and the next   one day

you will feel so

light and airy

your stomach will

uncoil

your face

unclench

and you will feel

like yourself

again.

Now I've let

that skunk dog in

that lurked on the porch

and it was just as bad

as I thought it

would be

but now it is time

to get rid of him

and go on

living and breathing

because I remember

learning to swim

in the dark water

without the tree,

without my Daddy's hand,

or the pink swimming ring.

And I guess if I can do that

I know how to sail above

the drowned leaves.

About the Author

"When I first started these poems," writes Ann Turner, "it was terribly painful, like eating ground glass. But at the same time, when they came pouring out of my heart and through my flying fingers, I felt washed, cleansed, and somehow renewed. These poems are a testimony to the healing power of words. In going back to my childhood, I remembered smells, sounds, the feel of the hot wood porch

under my feet, the look on my mother's face the day I told her. By taking something so painful and transforming it into words, rhythm, and images, the experience changed inside. Memories took on a cadence, almost a loveliness, so that it became a gift instead of a tragedy."

Ann Turner began her writing career as a poet and has subsequently published more than 35 critically acclaimed picture books, novels, and works of poetry for children and adults. Her distinguished backlist includes NETTIE'S TRIP SOUTH, FINDING WALTER, and GRASS SONGS. She lives with her husband and two children in Williamsburg, Massachusetts, where she tends her garden, takes long walks in the country with her dog, and writes full-time.

RAINN
RAPE, ABUSE & INCEST NATIONAL NETWORK
1-800-656-HOPE (1-800-656-4673)
http://www.rainn.org
FREE, 24-hour confidential counseling and
support for survivors of sexual assault. This
hotline connects callers confidentially with local
rape crisis center hotlines.

THE CHILDHELP USA® NATIONAL CHILD ABUSE HOTLINE
1-800-4-A-CHILD® (1-800-422-4453)
1-800-2-A-CHILD (T.D.D.)
http://www.childhelpusa.org
FREE, 24-hour hotline counselors offer
information and support for abused and
neglected children, parents, and professionals.

NATIONAL RUNAWAY SWITCHBOARD
1-800-621-4000
1-800-621-0394 (T.D.D.)
http://www.nrscrisisline.org
FREE, 24-hour confidential hotline for runaway
youth, teens in crisis, and concerned friends and
family members.